LORD
MANIFEST
BEFORE US

Mark Canada

CREATION
HOUSE

LORD MANIFEST BEFORE US: BALANCED BIBLICAL
INSIGHT ON CORPORATE WORSHIP
by Mark Canada
Published by Creation House
A Charisma Media Company
600 Rinehart Road
Lake Mary, Florida 32746
www.charismamedia.com

Unless otherwise noted, all Scripture quotations are from the King James Version of the Bible.

Scripture quotations marked NIV are from the Holy Bible, New International Version of the Bible. Copyright © 1973, 1978, 1984, International Bible Society. Used by permission.

Greek and Hebrew definitions taken from *The New Strong's Exhaustive Concordance of the Bible* (Carol Stream, IL: Thomas Nelson, 1990), and *A Hebrew and English Lexicon of the Old Testament, Including the Biblical Chaldee*, Wilhelm Gesenius (Boston: Crocker & Brewster, 1844).

Design Director: Bill Johnson
Cover design by Nathan Morgan

Visit the author's website:
www.ChristianLeviticalPraiseAndWorshipMinistries.org

Library of Congress Cataloging-in-Publication Data:
2012937902
International Standard Book Number: 978-1-62136-053-7
E-book International Standard Book Number:
978-1-62136-054-4

While the author has made every effort to provide
accurate telephone numbers and Internet addresses
at the time of publication, neither the publisher nor
the author assumes any responsibility for errors or for
changes that occur after publication.

First edition
12 13 14 15 16 — 987654321
Printed in the United States of America

Acknowledgments

I would like to acknowledge the following people and their impact on me in the area of corporate worship. First I want to thank Merle Sousa and his impact on teaching me the basic principles of worship while working with him at First Assembly of God in Fremont, California, and seeing strong prophetic worship when we were at Pleasanton Community Church in Pleasanton, California. Merle is a great music minister and worship leader. Second is my wife Patricia. While co-leading with her at Bethany Community Church in Stockton, California, we saw some great some moves of God. Third is Milo Miras and our years of leading worship at FGBM (Full Gospel Business Meetings) in the San Francisco Bay Area. Our group, Shepherd Fold, had some great worship experiences. Lastly, the worship seminars and conferences I attended. This list includes: International Worship Symposium in Pasadena, California, Shiloh Christian Fellowship Worship Conferences in Oakland, California, Integrity Hosanna Worship Conferences, Lamar Boschman Seminars and Kent Henry Seminars. Honors to my favorite conference speaker, Vivien Hibbert from the Worship Arts Conservatory of Woodland, California.

TABLE OF CONTENTS

BACKGROUND

Mᵧ ᴘᴜʀᴘᴏsᴇ ɪɴ this book is to share information that I have learned through the years being a church musician, attending fourteen worship conferences, and studying this subject on my own. I have been involved in a total of ten churches: two Baptist churches, a Mennonite church, two Assemblies of God churches, a Nazarene church, two Pentecostal churches, and two interdenominational churches. Within these churches, I have worked with twenty different worship leaders. These are great supplements in learning and experiencing God but they cannot take the place of the *Word* as our final authority of worship.

Nobody has the corner of worship but I believe we are all doing something right. We can learn from each other and eliminate what we are doing wrong. We need to be honest and compare our corporate worship with Scripture.

God will manifest in our churches if we will follow His biblical principles of worship, give Him an open window to respond, and have the passion for His presence. Pastors, worship leaders, and the congregation all have a role to bring this about. In this book, we will focus on the principles of worship, and the aim is to encourage churches to enter in more to worship God.

INTRODUCTION

A S MUCH AS we need daily prayer, Bible study, church attendance, and being involved in our churches, we also need the manifest presence of God in our worship services. The reasons for this will be answered in the following pages.

There are three types of the presence of God. One is the omnipresence of God, where God is everywhere. Second is the abiding presence of God. Third is the manifest presence of God, where He displays Himself. Even in the Old Testament, they had His abiding presence in the tabernacle of David, or more specifically in the ark of the covenant. David declares God's manifest presence where God inhabits the praises of His people, and in Psalm 24:7 and 9, "let the glory of God come in" (author's paraphrase). In the New Testament, the Holy Spirit abides with us and where two or more are gathered in His name, He is in the midst with us (Matt. 18:20). Then the manifest presence of God is displayed in Acts 2:42–43 with signs and wonders, and in Acts 16:25, where Paul and Silas were worshiping and then God created an earthquake. In 1 Corinthians, spiritual gifts were displayed.

I believe we will either see, hear, or sense His presence strongly when God manifests in our services. This should be the goal of worship, for it has a great purpose in our churches.

God uses signs and wonders (Acts 2:42–43), spiritual gifts (1 Cor. 12–14), and the prophetic arts—seen in the Book of Psalms—to manifest Himself in our assemblies. At the very minimum, we should be able to sense His presence strongly. We will go into the prophetic arts later.

The purpose of Him manifesting to us is to:

1. Draw us closer to Him in worship: "…and the glory of the LORD upon the house, they bowed themselves with their faces to the ground upon the pavement, and worshiped…" (2 Chron. 7:3).

2. Minister to us supernaturally: "But he that prophesieth speaketh unto men to edification, and exhortation, and comfort" (1 Cor. 14:3).

3. Deliver a sign to the unbeliever: "But if all prophesy, and there come in one that believeth not, or one unlearned, he is convinced of all, he is judged of all: And thus are the secrets of his

heart made manifest; and so falling
down on his face he will worship
God, and report that God is in you
of a truth" (1 Cor. 14:24–25); "And
He hath put a new song in my mouth,
even praise unto our God: many shall
see it, and fear, and shall trust in the
LORD" (Ps. 40:3).

I would like to say briefly here—and it is highly
important to know this—that there are obvious pre-
requisites before coming to worship. This is seen in
Acts 2:41–47 where they sold their goods and were in
one accord. Here we see the love and unity of the first
church. The Levites led worship in the Old Testament.
Their name in the Hebrew means to be in one accord.
David's tabernacle had unity.

Behold, how good and how pleasant it is for
brethren to dwell together in unity!
—PSALM 133:1

At Corinth we see the opposite where there is car-
nality and disunity. Although there were gifts displayed at Corinth, they were limited in power and
done improperly (1 Cor. 14).

Like any subject in the Bible, worship too must be
taken seriously. If we do not embrace the totality of
biblical worship, we are then incomplete as worshipers.

We do not pick what we like and discard what we do not like in the uses and principles of worship. Worship is a lot about bonding with God, and one of the main ways to love God in worship is to obey Him.

> If ye love me, keep my commandments.
> —JOHN 14:15

It does not matter the church label, type of music, or the liturgy, for He is "no respecter of persons" (Acts 10:34). The question is, are we being led by the Spirit and desiring His manifest presence?

We will now dive into the biblical principles of worship, Davidic worship, and the prophetic arts.

Chapter 1
PRINCIPLES OF WORSHIP

THERE ARE FOUR main principles of corporate worship. The first principle is "worshiping God in spirit and in truth" (John 4:24). The "truth" is Jesus (John 14:6) and the Word of God (John 17:17, "thy Word is truth"). The "spirit" has to do with our motivation, attitude and sincerity in our worship to God. In the context of this book of corporate worship, "spirit" has to do with the church humbling itself before God in what He wants for the worship service. We want to be sensitive to the Holy Spirit. The Bible says to "pray without ceasing" (1 Thess. 5:17); in other words, to be always in communication with God. Someone once said that if we are all Word, we dry up; and if we are all spirit, we blow up.[1] We must be balanced in our worship.

Worship is not all about plans nor is it all about hype. It is all about God and being scriptural. The second principle is, all things are to be done decently and in order (1 Cor. 14:40). "God is not the author of confusion" (1 Cor. 14:33). The manifest presence of God is not synonymous with being weird or wild.

God will not enter this type of artificial atmosphere according to the previous scriptures.

God looks at His church not being worshiped by many individuals, but as "one sound" (2 Chron. 5:13), "one mouth" (Rom. 15:6), and "one body" (1 Cor. 12:20). When you look at prophetic songs in 1 Chronicles 25:1-7, you see these under the direction of the captains, king, Asaph, Jeduthun, and Heman. The same we see in 1 Corinthians 14, where the prophetic was under the direction of Paul, the "order" and the display of the Spirit going hand in hand. A great sign of God that He is moving in our midst is if there is order in the display of the Spirit.

I have witnessed this on occasions. The error is when churches try to make things happen or churches that program every minute of the service where God is boxed out of the service.

The third principle of worship is the balance of song types in the service. The Bible says, "Let your moderation be known unto all men" (Phil. 4:5). I believe this is the most ignored principle in many of our churches. We are to sing "psalms and hymns and spiritual songs" (Eph. 5:19; Col. 3:16). Even in the Old Testament, they sang psalms, hymns, and new songs (spiritual songs). In the Book of Revelation, they sang new songs (Rev. 14:3), a psalm (song of Moses, Rev. 15:3) and a hymn (song of the Lamb, Rev. 15:3).

There are more commands to sing than to speak

or shout His praise. The only common way of worship that all churches do is singing. I personally believe singing is God's favorite form of expression that He wants from us. It is seen all over the Word and it is so much commanded. "Enter His gates with thanksgiving [lifted hands] and into His courts with praise [singing]" (Ps. 100:4). God inhabits the praises [singing] of His people (Ps. 22:3).

Notice the original meaning of the word *praise* in both of those scriptures. Since singing is a high priority with God, shouldn't we pay close attention to any commands pertaining to it?

Let us define the types of songs mentioned in the Bible. In the original Greek, a psalm is a sacred song, lyrics comprised of a teaching or scriptural quotation. A hymn is a testimonial song, like singing about what God has done or will do. A vast majority of music today in the church is by far the singing of hymns.

Relationship songs of love are under the hymn category. A new song or spiritual song is a non-rehearsed, spontaneous song. Sometimes it could be a prophetic song. The word *spiritual* for spiritual song in the Greek is *pneumatikos,* meaning spirit-breathed or spirit-initiated. The same word is seen in 1 Corinthians 12:1 for vocal gifts and 1 Corinthians 14:37 for prophetic gifts; a Holy Spirit-inspired song unto God. We will talk more about new songs later.

The key here is balance and not what is trendy

3

for the day. The recording industry does not set the standard of what to sing. It does not matter what is selling but instead what God wants in His church. I do not believe He wants us to be legalistic by doing 33 percent of each song type in a church service, but He does want all three somehow in the service. Why? Obviously, for balance and completeness. It would be like the pastor mostly preaching the grace of God and rarely the holiness of God.

> Let the word of Christ dwell in you richly in all wisdom; teaching and admonishing one another in psalms and hymns and spiritual songs.
>
> —COLOSSIANS 3:16

When we are singing, we are edifying each other by wisdom (spiritual songs), teaching (psalms), and admonishing (hymns). God-inspired prophetic songs give us wisdom for an individual or group at the time. Psalms teach us and hymns exhort or admonish us.

We need to know that our worship is going horizontal and vertical. God will respond to our worship more when we have this mental awareness that we are here for each other. Our worship is ministering to one another. It is not personal focus but group focus. God can and will touch us personally, but that is not the motive, because we can accomplish this by worshiping God alone.

The purpose of corporate worship is "we" centered, not "me" centered. We do not tune in and tune out, but tune in and be in tune with our corporate purpose in worship. Too much of church attendance is based on getting something rather than on giving, using our talents, time, money—and yes, our worship—to edify one another. When worshiping corporately, we need to focus on wanting God to minister to individuals who need salvations, healings, and deliverances. One of the main tenets of the kingdom of God is putting others first, and God will bless us when we do. This is why we come together to worship God as a group. There is also that corporate purpose of God wanting to do something in the services that will benefit us all as a local body. We all need to be on the same boat listening to the Spirit's call because God wants to use us all to accomplish this.

This leads us to the fourth and final principle, and that is the prophetic. Typically God uses this medium to manifest Himself. Prophecy is simply what God is saying now for emphasis. It could even be a scripture that God has laid on someone's heart to tell someone. When a Christian says, "I feel led to..." or "You came to mind today...," that is the prophetic in motion. When we follow through, God then gives us the right words to say at the time. A word in due season. This gives God the glory, for we know this is an unusual event, and we see the purpose of it as it helps and ministers to the person being spoken to.

God wants to speak and respond to our worship. After or during the worship, we need to be sensitive to what He might do. David says, "Praise waiteth for thee, O God" (Ps. 65:1). In Psalm 68:24–25, it states, "[I] have seen thy goings...in the sanctuary." Psalm 77:13 says, "Have thy way in the sanctuary" (author's paraphrase). For example, during a time of meditation after the singing, someone can stand and simply say that he or she feels God is wanting to say that He loves us. Of course this would be something that he would sense God wanting him or her to say. There are people in the congregation that maybe really needed to here that for an encouragement or comfort.

> But he that prophesieth speaketh unto men to edification, and exhortation, and comfort.
>
> —1 Corinthians 14:3

"The prophetic plans and the prophetic is always listening during the plan."[2] Is our trust in the plan or in God? We are always to be dependent on Him 24/7 even if we know God has given the plan. His will can change anytime in anyway. Are we willing to yield to that?

Chapter 2
DAVIDIC WORSHIP

NOW LET US go into how God wants us to worship Him and that is through Davidic worship, or more specifically, the Book of Psalms. Here are some of the simple facts on why we need to follow Psalms in our worship services.

Psalms is the most quoted book in the New Testament and the largest book in the Bible. Every book in the Bible has a theme and many scholars believe the theme of Psalms is worship. It is our only handbook on worship. In the New Testament, Corinth is our bad example and the tabernacle of David is our good one. Obviously, God would want us to follow the good example of worship.

Paul used the Old Testament to worship (Acts 24:14). Davidic worship is seen in heaven: "shout" in Psalm 32:11 and Revelation 7:10; "loud noise" in Psalm 33:3 and Revelation 4:5, instruments in Psalm 150:3–5 and Revelation 8:2; 15:2; "singing" in Psalm 47:6 and Revelation 15:3; "banners" in Psalm 20:5; 60:4 and Revelation 7:9 (palm leaves), "new songs" in Psalm 96:1 and Revelation 5:9; 14:3; "standing" in Psalm

135:2 and Revelation 7:9; "dance" in Psalm 149:3 and Revelation 19:7 (rejoice); "kneeling" in Psalm 95:6 and Revelation 19:10; and finally, Hallal praise (great display) in Psalm 68:24–25 and Revelation 4:3–6 (sounds and colors in heaven).

What about lifted hands and clapping? Whenever clapping is mentioned in the Old Testament it is usually in context with spiritual warfare, and none of that is going on in heaven. Lifted hands are always going up to the atmosphere, and in heaven God is right there before us when we worship, so there is no need to do so. God loves to "indwell" this type of worship, as stated in Psalm 132:13–14: "For the Lord hath chosen Zion; He hath desired it for His habitation. This is my rest for ever: here will I dwell; for I have desired it." "But chose the tribe of Judah, the mount Zion which he loved" (Ps. 78:68). "But ye are come unto mount Zion, and unto the city of the living God, the heavenly Jerusalem..." (Heb. 12:22).

For those who say the New Testament is the only form we need to follow today, then we are all disobedient because we all sometimes stand in our worship. Standing is not commanded or seen in the worship of the New Testament church. Only singing, dancing, and lifted hands are mentioned in the New Testament. We need to follow the whole counsel of God and not use dispensational theories to support our positions.

These gestures and performing arts done in the Old

Testament church were not commanded to be done only in a cultural matter. David never implied that we are to sing Jewish songs, play Jewish instruments, or do Jewish dances to worship. Throughout time, cultures around the world used many of these biblical forms of praise in their own way in annual festivals, ceremonies, and religious rituals. I truly believe God has programmed some of these ways of worship for the main purpose of worshiping Him. Look at many concerts that we see today.

Look at the reactions of people to the music. You see clapping, shouting, dancing, hands lifted, singing, and girls crying out. They are in a sense worshiping the artist and/or the music being performed. Their whole body is involved in their response. We see this with crowds at sporting events. Davidic worship is expressive, prophetic, and versatile, displaying itself in two main ways.

The first way is the various moods of worship. In the Hebrew, the word *praise* has different meanings, from kneeling to shouting. In the Book of Psalms, we see solemn worship (Psalm 95:6, "O come, let us worship and bow down: let us kneel before the LORD our maker"); celebratory worship (Psalm 98:4, "Make a joyful noise unto the LORD, all the earth: make a loud noise, and rejoice, and sing praise"); warfare worship (Psalm 47 and Psalm 149:6, "Let the high praises of God be in their mouth, and a two-edged sword in their hand"); crying out worship (Psalm 28:2, "Hear the voice of my supplications, when I cry unto thee, when I lift up my hands toward thy holy oracle"); and intimate worship (Psalm 27:4, "One thing have I desired of the LORD, that will I seek after; that I may dwell in the house of the LORD all the days of my life, to behold the beauty of the LORD, and to enquire in his temple")

We need to be Spirit-led, what God wants, and not camp out on one of the moods based on tradition or personal preference. God is not into religion, tradition, or rituals, but instead desires from us variety, excellence, creativity, and uniqueness in our worship. We go all out for weddings, anniversaries, birthdays, and graduations. So how about God? This does not mean we try to be different every time, but neither do we dismiss anything new and different to what the church is used to. As long as it is not immoral, unethical, or against foundational Christian doctrine, we should be open.

I remember visiting a church in Anaheim, California, where they met in an old circus arena. On the bottom floor was the worship team and on the side of the stage were two large water fountains. While the worship was playing, the fountains would correspond to the music. The louder the song, the higher the water went. The thrust pulse of water between each fountain was predicated upon the tempo of the song.

It really enhanced the worship, much like music does to the lyrics of a song. Even though water fountains are not mentioned in the Word and there are no water fountain classes in worship seminars, this still does not weaken the validity of something unique a church can do in worship. We will get into this more later on, the visual enhancement of worship.

The second display of Davidic worship is the various gestures and performing arts in the sanctuary. The gestures we see are lifted hands (Ps. 134:2), clapping (Ps. 47:1), bowing (Ps. 95:6), and standing (Ps. 135:2). The performing arts we see are dance teams (Ps. 149:3, in the Hebrew), banner teams (Ps. 20:5), singers, tambourines, processions and instrumentalists (Ps. 68:25). I know a few of these are controversial. We will answer these questions later.

There are a few broad comments I would like to mention about these in our practical uses. Unless specifically told to be done in a certain way by the leader, make your gestures personal. Sometimes God wants uniformity and sometimes He wants unity with diversity.

> Shout unto God with the voice of triumph.
> —Psalm 47:1

Shout what? He gives us liberty to shout whatever. The point of this scripture was to be loud. The unity was the volume and the diversity was the word

11

content. When the leader wants us to clap, do not feel you have to clap a certain way. A side note here about leaders is we must give them the benefit of a doubt that they are being led by God. Whether they verbalize a wanting to worship God a certain way or if they pick a song that has a certain gesture like clapping or bowing in the lyrics, we must follow through and obey. God knows the lyrics when He impresses upon the worship leader to pick a certain song for that Sunday.

If we do not trust our leaders, then everything is open for questions. I have never experienced a worship leader asking us to do something anti-biblical. They get very frustrated when they know they are hearing from God and the congregation does not follow through. They either get self-conscious about how to do it or give up altogether. I know because I have worked with many of them. We need to make their leadership easier and just go with the flow in what they want. Sometimes it is a sacrifice of praise for us to do something uncomfortable in praise and worship.

Don't you think God will receive that response more than us just going through the motions with gestures we are comfortable with? Do them your own personal way. This will make your worship more intimate.

There is a measure of art in all of us. God will never

command us to do something we could not do. God wants the beginners to the advanced to participate in the performing arts. He commands us to "sing" (Ps. 33:2), "make a joyful noise" (Ps. 66:1; 98:4), "dance" (Ps. 149:3), and "sing new songs" (Ps. 33:3).

We are not all soloists, but we can all sing. Even those that are monotone can be easily taught to sing. There is not a big difference between a gifted singer (soloist) and a singer who is not, if they are trained the same musically.

We idolize artists way too much in our world today. Yes, we respect and honor their training and experience, but God looks at the character and the sensitivity to Him when they are performing.

We can all make a joyful noise. Even a six-year-old can keep a tempo and knows the harder you hit an object, the louder its volume will be. Tempo and volume are a part of art. I know if I were to give out a legitimate percussion instrument like a tambourine to a congregation, they would be able to play it easily by keeping a tempo to the song. It is very rare to see someone clap off tempo when people clap to a song.

We can all sing a new song or spiritual song unto God. You do not have to be a songwriter to do this effectively. David commanded his congregation to sing new songs (Ps. 33:3). Paul commanded the churches at Ephesus (Eph. 5:19) and Colossia (Col. 3:16) to sing spiritual songs.

A new song is not defined by what a current song is defined by today's standards. It does not have to have an intro, verses, chorus, and bridge. The recording industry does not set the standard. It is a good source for psalms and hymns, but not for spontaneous songs unto God. New songs come personally from the worshiper where his or her own melodies and lyrics create the song.

It can even be chant-like in its nature. The earliest form of singing was the chant. New songs or spiritual songs are the most intimate and simplistic forms of singing to God because they come from you and not from a writer you do not even know.

Lastly, we can all dance. I will go into this in detail later.

My last broad comment on gestures is that the listing in the Bible is not the maximum amount we can use in our services. This is the starting point and the minimum that I believe God wants from us. Just because some activity or performing art is not mentioned in the Word, does not mean then it is wrong, sinful, or anti-biblical to use it. God will receive any action of worship to Him as long as it does not disobey a principle or specific command, and is out not of context with the mood at the time. We do many things in the church that are not mentioned in the Bible, like Sunday School, fund raisers, church office procedures, announcements, bulletins, specific ministries to age and gender groups (men's ministry, youth, and so forth), and altar calls—all activities that God blesses, and are needed.

These strengthen the church. The church is more powerful when we use current technologies and are culturally relevant in communicating the gospel. In worship you see people pace, close eyes, look up, do cat calls, fold hands, wave white handkerchiefs, sway, whistle, and hum. God receives these un-biblical ways as much as the biblical ones because it is the heart of worship that matters. Non-biblical is not synonymous with anti-biblical. That does not mean we accept everything because biblical principles will guide us. For example, belly dancing is a legitimate dance art form but it cannot be done in the church because of what the Word says about sensuality. It is a sensual dance. The Bible talks about dressing modestly (1 Tim. 2:9). Singers should not wear revealing or tight outfits anywhere in public, yet alone in church. An example of something being out of context in a service is someone shouting and jumping during a solemn time of worship. This would be very distracting and would draw a lot of attention to that person's action rather than to God.

Who sets the standard, and by what authority? The Bible and the liberty God gives us.

Chapter 3
DANCING, BANNERS
& NEW SONGS

IT IS INTERESTING to notice that in the Bible it does not say that God claps over us, kneels over us, stands over us, shouts over us, or even plays an instrument over us. We do know that His banner over us is love (Song of Sol. 2:4) and He sings and dances over us ("…He will rejoice over thee with joy [*leaping* in the Hebrew]. He will rest in His love, He will joy over thee with singing"). We will see in this chapter how God uses these arts to display Himself. I know there are many questions on these three topics so I will try to answer some of them in this chapter.

Let us start first with dancing. Dancing is movements and steps with time in music. This art form is all over the Word. It is in the Old Testament, New Testament, and is seen in heaven. In Psalm 149:3 and Psalm 150:4 we are commanded to dance in worship to God. In the original language, it also includes dance teams. Many people do not realize that the words *rejoice*, *great gladness*, and *exceeding joy* in the original Greek mean literally to dance. In fact, many times the word *rejoice* means to dance. In Acts 3:8, a lame man just healed was leaping (form of dance) in the temple during a meeting. There is no hint of this being disrespectful in the house of God. This is a typical reaction when one was joyful in biblical times and in many cultures today. We too in this country would dance if our team won the Super Bowl or if we won the lottery. Why are not we this way with God? Even in heaven there will be dancing. In Revelation 19:7, the word *rejoice* means "to dance" in the Greek. Two other times in Revelation 12:12 and 18:20, *rejoice* is mentioned. In the original language, the meaning is to make merriment. This to me strongly implies singing and dancing.

There are three types of dance in the Bible, and they are twirling, jumping or leaping, and group dancing. Notice the different stages from beginning to more advanced. Everyone cannot twirl, but anyone can surely jump or leap. The group dance teams were either processional or were circle dance teams. Swaying could also be a form of dance. It is not limited to twirling or jumping. The practicality of dancing in corporate worship is that you do not need an open area of the church to dance before Him. A jump or sway could be done right where you are at in the seating aisle. No need to be highly flexible and coordinated to dance before God.

If you have not yet, I encourage you to enter in

to this art form in worship, for you will see more freedom and intimacy with God when you do. For further reading on this subject read *Rejoice: A Biblical Study of the Dance*, by Debbie Roberts.[1]

What about banner and flag teams? First I would like to mention that there is no command in Scripture to implement flags and banners in worship services, but it is a tool of worship seen in the Word. In Psalm 20:2-5, the phrase "set up our banners" means literally to lift up banners. Banners and flags were made for movement either by the natural wind or those holding them. The movement and colors symbolize either what God is doing in our midst (prophetic) or are just simply used to embellish the worship service. In Revelation 7:9, palm leaves were waving in worship: "A great multitude...stood before the throne, and before the Lamb, clothed with white robes, and palms in their hands." The original Greek for *palms* here means grasping an instrument. An instrument is not statutory, but implies movement. It is used for something.

Banners and flags come under a larger area of a display of art in the sanctuary. The Hebrew command for *praise* can sometimes mean *Hallal*.

Hallal means to make a great display. This can be statutory or movement art in the sanctuary. We see this in Exodus 25:2-8 with Moses's temple with colors, metals, precious stones, horns, and a cherub;

in 1 Chronicles 22:5 with Solomon's temple, a house that must be magnificent of fame and glory, described in detail in 2 Chronicles 3–4; in Revelation 4:3–5 with the throne of God being surrounded by colors, lamps, and sounds; in Psalm 68:24–25, with tambourine teams and processions; and in Psalm 150:4, dance teams. In addition, today we see multimedia presentations, mime teams and prophetic painting. It is up to the pastor what to display where, when, and how. Something needs to be done, though, for it is a command in the Word.

The main purpose of art is to bring glory to God, whether it is a fine art or a performing art. As music embellishes the lyrics, visual art teams embellish the music and the lyrics. It is so easy to be distracted when you are just singing; but when the visual is involved, you then become more involved. That is because more of your body is now being involved.

Seeing and acting out the visual of any song brings you into the worship more than you realize. You have to really experience this to appreciate it. You focus much more.

I want to now go into an expansion of new songs or spiritual songs. As I mentioned before, this is a spontaneous, non-rehearsed song unto God. Any believer can do this. In Psalm 33:3, 96:1, 98:1, and 149:1, we are all commanded to sing "new songs."

Sometimes, God will give a song to someone, who

will then sing it, and then we learn it to sing back to God. I have seen this several times in services. The multimedia person has to be quick to type the song as it is being sung by the soloist so we can pick it up right away. We see two examples of this in Scripture. Deuteronomy 31:19 says, "Now therefore write ye this song for you, and teach it the children of Israel: put it in their mouths, that this song may be a witness for me against the children of Israel." In Revelation 14:3, we see it again when they sang a new song that they only can learn. Either someone sang it and the crowd learned it, or it was done simultaneously.

These new songs take us to a supernatural level of worship because we are drawing closer to God in intimacy, for the songs are coming from us. I was part of a worship team that traveled around playing at Full Gospel Business Meetings (FGBM). During one meeting in San Pablo, California, we did a worship service. After the main singing was done, we immediately went into spiritual songs unto God done without instruments. Within minutes of singing these, we suddenly all sensed to get gradually softer. No one was leading this. Silence then came, and later a prophetic word was given. The congregation was working together with the Holy Spirit. God draws near when we draw near. Hebrews 10:21–22 says, "Having a high priest over the house of God; let us draw near." James 4:8 says, "Draw nigh to God, and he will draw nigh to you." New songs are one of the main ways of drawing near to God.

There are more commands to sing new songs and spiritual songs than psalms and hymns. I believe God likes the more intimate songs of worship. According to Psalm 40:3, even unbelievers will sense God's presence and repent when new songs are sung: "And He hath put a new song in my mouth, even praise unto my God, many will see it, and fear, and shall trust in the Lord." Personally when I am in a gathering where most of the congregation is singing new songs and not hurrying on to finish the worship portion of the service, there is a level of worship that is quite incredible. Musically, this is the climax of the worship service. Everything else seems so anticlimactic.

On the practical level, new songs or spiritual songs are done in the service usually when the worship leader tells us to continue to worship after the song has ended, or if nothing is said and the music continues. That is our cue to enter in. Just start singing. You will usually start singing just one or two notes, but after that, you will become more proficient as you proceed in this each Sunday.

I would like to share one more experience with you. In his book, *90 Minutes in Heaven,* the author, Don Piper, a Baptist pastor, tells of his near-death experience. He was pronounced dead by paramedics after a car crash he had in Texas. While he was in heaven, he mentions that the worship there was wonderful. Everyone was singing different songs simultaneously and he said it was incredibly harmonic. He had never heard anything like this on earth.[2] We can have a sample of this when we sing new songs or spiritual songs together. He is right. Despite different songs being sung, there is a beautiful harmony. This cannot be done in the natural but is Holy Spirit driven. In the secular arena, this would sound chaotic.

Another type of new song is the prophetic song, or Song of the Lord. We will go into this later in chapter four, "The Prophetic Arts."

Chapter 4
THE PROPHETIC ARTS

God is in the midst of our music, but He
works through our music.

—LAMAR BOSCHMAN,
The Rebirth of Music[1]

WHEN THE ARTIST does his or her art unto
God, it then becomes prophetic. The one that
is seeing or hearing the art then becomes God-con-
scious. We do not center on the art or the artist, but
instead on God. If you were to visit the great cathe-
drals of Europe, you could not help but to think about
God and His majesty. The difference between a secular artist and a Christian artist should be the motivation behind our art display. We want to display
God, and the secular artist wants to display his or her
talent. The Christian artist does not rely mainly on
talent, experience, or training when displaying the art,
but instead on God. This will then make it prophetic.

I am not impressed anymore by the performance of someone, but instead, if he is relying God. If he is, then we will draw closer to God during the art display. A common way we see in Scripture where God manifests is through the performing arts. We will go into three areas: the voice of God, the sound of God, and the sight of God.

Most prophecies were sung in the Bible. We know that because prophecies were typically accompanied by musical instruments (2 Kings 3:11–16; 1 Sam. 10:5–6), and the meter of the prophecy strongly implies this. The Book of Psalms is mainly a collection of prophetic songs by David and others that were moved by the Holy Spirit. These songs were recorded as a part of Holy Scripture because of the prophetic content of the songs. A specific example of this is Psalm 22:17–18, where soldiers were gambling for Jesus's coat. This was fulfilled in Matthew 27:35–36.

Zephaniah 3:17 says He will joy over thee with singing. A Messianic psalm speaking of the Lord in Psalm 22:22 says, "In the midst of the congregation will I praise thee." This is again mentioned in Hebrews 2:12 (NIV), "In the presence of the congregation will I sing your praises." In context, the one spoken in the first person is Jesus.

Research has shown that between something that is said and something that is sung, the latter has a stronger impact on the listeners, and they retain more of the content.[2] A strong example of that are commercials. I can still remember cigarette commercials of the 1970s. They used melodic jingles with their messages for a bigger impact of retention. What has Satan used from the 1960s to today to preach his message of drugs, sex, alcohol, and rebellion? The medium of rock and roll music.

Martin Luther and Charles Wesley used music to teach biblical truths. They knew the impact music had on people. So if you combined music with the prophetic, one can imagine the impact this can have, and why God did it this way.

> The Song of the Lord [prophetic song] is a spiritual song directed primarily to God's people as the singer becomes a channel for the Lord to convey a message in song.
>
> —DR. DAVID BLOMGREN,
> *The Song of the Lord*[3]

I would like to show some powerful examples of prophetic songs today in the church. My wife and I have several times visited a church in Oakland, California, called Shiloh Christian Fellowship. This is a church of about one thousand people, and they have a standing mic in front of the stage for anyone who feels led to give a prophetic song. The times that we have been there, they average two to three people per service giving prophetic songs. Keep in mind the singer has no idea what key or chord progression the band is playing. The decency and the order of the Holy Spirit brings it all together. The songs were in perfect range for the singer and the melodies complimented the chord progression. This happened every time we went. You can tell by the quality of their voices these singers were not soloists. On paper, this really cannot happen in any other scenario other than a group of hungry worshipers.

A prophetic worship seminar I have attended many times always has prophetic songs in the services, but this one time was quite miraculous. One singer started to sing and then sporadically the other three joined in. Soon we had four singers singing melodically and lyrically the same thing. In addition to this marvel, when I turned to my wife to comment, she said she knew where they were going musically and lyrically. Why? Because she was plugged in spiritually. How could she know this in the natural? She did not know these people nor did she ever rehearse with them. I say that because you can develop a sense of where people are going when you work with them a lot, although this would be hard to do lyrically in a spontaneous song. This was a supernatural event.

The next area is the sound of God.

> David and the captains of the host separated to the service of the sons of Asaph,

and of Heman, and of Jeduthun, who
should prophesy with harps, with psalteries,
and with cymbals.

—1 CHRONICLES 25:1

Under the hands of their father Jeduthun,
who prophesied with a harp.

—1 CHRONICLES 25:3

God is... [in] the sound of a trumpet.

—PSALM 47:5

Prophetic instrumentalists can deliver with their
sound:

And it came to pass, when the evil spirit
from God was upon Saul, that David took a
harp, and played with his hand: so Saul was
refreshed, and was well, and the evil spirit
departed from him.

—1 SAMUEL 16:23

Prophetic sounds will prepare us to hear the Word:

As you approach the town, you will meet a
procession of prophets, coming down from
the high place with lyres, tambourines,
flutes and harps being played before them,
and they will be prophesying.

—1 SAMUEL 10:5, NIV

> But now bring me a minstrel. And it came
> to pass, when the minstrel played, that the
> hand of the LORD came upon him [Elisha]
> And he said, Thus saith the LORD...
>
> —2 KINGS 3:15–16

> And when the burnt offering began, the
> song of the LORD began also with the trum-
> pets, and with the instruments ordained by
> David.
>
> —2 CHRONICLES 29:27

As you can see with these verses, the musician can have just as much of an influence prophetically in a worship service as a singer. He just needs to come with a clean heart and to be sensitive to what the Holy Spirit wants in the service.

I was a main keyboardist at a church in Pleasanton, California. At one of our services, we were singing spiritual songs at the beginning of the service. I remember running out of ideas while I was playing, and then asking the Lord for something new to play with the singing. Within seconds, I started to play something very simple, and very soon after that, the congregation got louder and more intense in their singing. I did not get any louder and did not play more intensely with more piano technique. God was working through my instrument when I yielded to Him. It is so easy as a gifted, trained, and experienced performing artist to be dependent on our training. A true Christian artist should always depend on God. We too have to "pray without ceasing" when playing or singing (1 Thess. 5:17). This is the difference between a secular artist and a Christian artist. The decency and order of the Holy Spirit was exhibited in that service because the key we were doing the spiritual songs in was the same key of our first song of the set. These new songs at the beginning of the service were initiated by the pastor and not by a singer.

The current church I attend now in Stockton, California, is called Lifesong. I was playing some percussion instruments during one of the services, and before the service I remember praying for God to use me how He wanted to that day. This should be the prayer of every artist before the services of their churches.

We were singing the song "I Exalt Thee" by Pete Sanchez when in the middle of the song our pastor got up on the stage and said he was sensing God wanted to release peace on us. While he was speaking, I was sensing that God wanted me to play the wind chimes in a slow descending pattern five times. When he said to receive it now, I then began to play. I paused about three seconds each time I did a pattern. After the fifth time, he moved on with the service. This was a special time that the Holy Spirit used our pastor and the sound of God to help us receive His peace being poured upon us. I did not realize until later that God's number of grace is the number five. Pastor James did not enter back in again until the fifth pattern was done. It was timed perfectly. Two people were just sensitive to the Holy Spirit. Although it looked planned, we knew it was initiated by God.

Lastly, there is the sight of God. All through the Word, we see God in many typologies. God is in the wind, fire, cloud, and smoke, to name just a few. God is also seen in the visual performing arts. Psalm 68:24–25 shows a spontaneous procession spurred on by God. The Bible called this "a going of God," a procession consisting of singers, musicians, and a tambourine team, the spontaneous and the orderly working hand in hand. Dancing too can be a sight of God where God works through a dancer. He will rejoice over you with joy (*leap* or *dance* in the Hebrew)(Zeph. 3:17).

A worship leader that I was working with mentioned to me a desire he had for a song he planned for the service entitled "Lift High the Lord Our Banner" by Macon Delavan. He wanted our flag team to do a planned procession through our congregation. Well, it fell through because he did not get a chance to talk to the flag leader. When we sang the song in the service, our pastor started to march through the congregation. Then my wife grabbed a Lion of Judah flag and marched with him. One by one, others joined in the procession. We had a "going of God" in our church. Our pastor did not know the desire of the worship leader, but he did know the desire of God and went with the flow of the Holy Spirit. God was showing us that He did not want it planned, but instead wanted it done prophetically. God got the glory.

At Shiloh Christian Fellowship in Oakland, California, we attended a service where we were singing a medley of Jewish songs. While we were singing, people got up sporadically to dance a circle dance around the inside perimeter of the sanctuary. It was made up of children, parents, seniors, short people, and tall people. When performed, it looked well rehearsed, but visually it looked wrong because of height variances of the people. It came together poorly at the start, but in a short time it really came together. After that, it looked very well rehearsed.

If this were planned, it would have started out much more professionally. God just put it together. Another "going of God" was done that day.

God can move upon prophetic painters in a service. At a worship conference I attended, there were four easels of painting canvasses near the stage for anyone to use in the service. This one service I will never forget. Again, while we were worshiping, three people got up and started painting crosses as their center-piece. Just seconds after this was done, we started to sing songs about the cross.

Later in the service, we had a dance special and a flag special with the cross as the theme. These artists were people from the crowd and did not know the plans for the service. God just brought it all together with the planned and the prophetic.

Lastly, I would like to share the most incredible going of God I have ever witnessed. At this same worship conference, the leader sensed that God wanted us to worship Him as our Warrior. During the time that he was talking, the visual art teams met separately with their leaders. You could see this live happening offstage. These teams were made up of delegates or attendees of the conference.

These leaders were communicating to them the visuals they saw from God during the worship. Keep in mind the leaders were not communicating with the other leaders at any time. There is an open space area before the stage for people to dance and wave flags during worship. This is where the art teams (mime, dance, and flags) came together in a spontaneous production unto God. They were all embellishing the theme at that time and we were singing with them. I have been in many plays and musicals in and outside the church; what I saw then could not happen in the natural without many rehearsals. Even if this were planned, it would have taken more weeks than a weekend conference for this to come off so professionally. With exception of the mime team, all the teams had inexperienced members in them. The workshops were the only times they met, and during that time, they went over the special numbers for the evening service. You are really put on the spot when this happens because you never rehearse where to go.

As I have mentioned earlier, the visual really enhances the worship service. When you're just singing, it is so easy to de distracted or even daydream, especially if you are singing a phrase over and over again. The visual gives you a finer picture of what you are communicating to God in worship. I believe this is why God uses this medium to help us.

Chapter 5
SIGNS AND WONDERS

IN THIS CHAPTER, we will show the connection of signs and wonders in the context of worship, listing current illustrations. As you know, signs and wonders are numerous throughout the Bible and reported throughout church history. Let us look at three examples:

> It came even to pass, as the trumpeters and singers were as one, to make one sound to be heard in praising and thanking the LORD; and when they lifted up their voice with the trumpets and cymbals and instruments of music, and praised the LORD, saying, For he is good; for his mercy endureth forever: that then the house was filled with a cloud, even the house of the LORD. So that the priests could not stand to minister by reason of the cloud: for the glory of the LORD had filled the house of God.
>
> —2 CHRONICLES 5:13–14

And they continued steadfastly in the apostles' doctrine and fellowship, and in breaking of bread, and in prayers. And fear came upon every soul: and many wonders and signs were done by the apostles... Praising God, and having favor with all the people.

—ACTS 2:42–43, 47

And at midnight Paul and Silas prayed, and sang praises unto God: and the prisoners heard them. And suddenly there was a great earthquake, so that the foundations of the prison were shaken: and immediately all the doors were opened, and every one's bands were loosed.

—ACTS 16:25–26

It is obvious to see here that worship plays in the development of the manifest presence of God. In churches today where there is a great move of God, the worship is usually no less than forty-five minutes. We cannot rush in and out of God's presence. In these three examples, we see signs and wonders.

I would like to share with you now some illustrations that happened recently. The first is when I was discussing an incident in the Bible called the Shekinah glory with a pastor I knew. As soon as I brought it up, he immediately recalled an account

35

that had happened to him. He told it like it had just happened yesterday.

While in the jungles of the Philippines, this pastor was having a church service in a small village building. During the worship, a purple mist came in and filled the building. The congregation simultaneously fell to their knees and went into fervent worship. This is an example of the manifest presence of God drawing people to more intimate worship.

A second event happened in San Jose, California, at Calvary Community Church. During an evangelistic crusade, a cloud descended on top of the church and hovered over it. People driving by the church were testifying to the event. Out of curiosity, many stopped and went into the church. There were many salvations; so many that a church was birthed. That church is still here today. Jubilee Christian Center is one of the largest churches in the San Francisco Bay Area. This was the manifest presence of God bringing salvations.

The last event happened to my wife at a Benny Hinn crusade. During the worship, Pastor Hinn turned around and faced the choir. My wife was in that choir. He then waved his arm over them. Like dominoes, they fell under the power of the Holy Spirit. She then felt the palms of hands becoming very hot. This lasted for a few days after the crusade. She sensed the purpose was for laying hands on individuals who needed physical healing. She knew someone who needed healing, so she went to that person and prayed over her. She was healed. This was the manifest presence of God used for ministry.

All of these instances came from nowhere in the natural and unexpectedly. All had spiritual purposes and were the results of worship to God.

CONCLUSION

WE CANNOT ALWAYS assume that when a manifestation occurs, the source is always God. Especially when individuals react to "God's presence" in a worship service. We can easily work up our emotions or try to imitate an experience that we think has to occur. Another example can be autosuggestion, where we are told what is the correct experience to have and we obey. A lot of this is done innocently with the individual not knowing this is not how God works.

I will share two experiences in two different churches that I have observed concerning this. I remember visiting a church where the pastor was praying over a man with a very bad limp. He very gingerly walked up to the front of the church for prayer. After the prayer, he walked normally. When I saw him in the parking lot just before the service ended, the very bad limping had returned. This temporary healing most likely could have been a result of adrenaline. I believe when he was being prayed for, he got himself so excited that adrenaline removed much of the pain and allowed him to walk normally. I also believe physical healings of God are not short-lived.

In another church that I attended, a healing came miraculously. We knew a lady who used a walker. During the worship service, she testified that she had been healed. She walked normally again many months afterwards.

For my own personal experience, I had one fake and one actual experience from God. Others and I were being prayed for in front of a gathering at a FGBM meeting. Those being prayed for before me were falling down or being "slain in the Spirit." Nothing was happening to me when I was being prayed for, so I faked falling down so I would not embarrass the speaker or myself. When you are standing up with your eyes closed, you have a natural tendency to lose your balance, for your body is disoriented. I believe some people think it is the Holy Spirit doing this, when in reality it is the natural reaction of your body. Another time I was being prayed over when suddenly I completely lost all my balance and fell backwards. It was as if my legs turned into Jell-O. I also saw a bright light in my vision even though my eyes were closed.

In 1 Thessalonians 5:21, we are commanded to "test everything" (NIV). First John 4:1 says we are to "test the spirits" (NIV). Paul commended the Bereans for testing what he was preaching to them by comparing his content with Scripture. We are not to be gullible nor are we to be cynical. There are usually two schools of thoughts when it comes to experiences and unusual events in the church. One says that it is manmade or demonic, and the other says it is always of God because of the church environment.

If we have presuppositions like this, then there is no reason to test. We are then saying these commands in the Bible are invalid because we already made up our minds on the matter. Some say it is too weird to be of God, and others say it is so weird it must be God. It is not based upon what is normal or abnormal in our church, but we must ask, Is it biblical, and is it in order with the mood of worship? Are we beholden to tradition, religion, and legalism, or are we open and testing what is before us?

To those in mainline churches, I want to encourage you to allow God to move in your services. Give Him some time to respond to the worship. Biblical worship is not tied to the type of music, church label, or type of liturgy (program) used. For a good variety, allow more creative arts to be used in the worship. Give other performing artists a chance to use their gifts for God like what is done already with singers and musicians.

To Pentecostal and Charismatic churches, we need to realize that we do not need to hype the crowd or get them emotionally worked up like we see in rock concerts. There is a difference between encouraging people to enter more into worship and hyping people up. These churches are strong in being expressive and letting God move prophetically, but we have traditions also that we need to let go. A Spirit-led church needs to be led by the Spirit and not be camping out on one of the moods of worship, whether crying out or celebratory worship. We must be open for all of them.

As I mentioned earlier at the beginning of the book, we are all doing some things right but need to be open for improvements in our worship. We can never be satisfied in our level of worship, or we will be just going through the motions.

There is so much more of God. We do not seek experiences but we do want His manifest presence to change people and give direction in our services. Let us be biblical and learn from each other. I hope the training I received, experiences, and personal study have helped you to move higher in worship. My prayer is for all churches to see, hear, or strongly sense His manifest presence. God bless you all.

APPENDIX

OLD TESTAMENT AND HEAVEN WORSHIP

Singing

- Psalm 47:6: "Sing praises to God…"

- Revelation 15:3: "And they sing the song of Moses…and the song of the Lamb."

Shouting

- Psalm 32:11: "…and shout for joy…"

- Revelation 7:10: "Cried with a loud voice…"

Loud Noise

- Psalm 33:3: "…play skillfully with a loud noise…"

- Revelation 4:5: "And out of the throne proceeded lightnings and thunderings…"

Instruments

- Psalm 150:3: "Praise Him with sound of the trumpet: praise him with the psaltery and harp"

- Revelation 15:2: "...stand on the sea of glass, having the harps of God."

Banners

- Psalm 20:5 "We will rejoice...and we will set up [lift up] our banners..."

- Revelation 7:9 "...a great multitude...holding palm branches in their hands [grasping an instrument]."

New Songs

- Psalm 96:1: "Sing unto the LORD a new song..."

- Revelation 5:9: "and they sang a new song..." (NIV).

Standing

- Psalm 135:2: "Ye that stand in the house of the LORD."

- Revelation 7:9 "...a great multitude...stood before the throne..."

Kneeling

- Psalm 95:6: "Let us worship and bow down: let us kneel..."

- Revelation 5:14: "...four and twenty elders fell down and worshiped..."

Dancing

- Psalm 149:3: "Let them praise his name in the dance..."

- Revelation 19:7: "Let us be glad and rejoice [*dance* in the Greek], and give honor to Him..."

Hallal Praise (Great display)

- Psalm 68:24–25: "They have seen thy goings, O God...in the sanctuary. The singers went before, the players of instruments followed after; among them were the damsels playing with timbrels."

- Revelation 4:3–6: "jasper...sardine stone...rainbow round about the throne...emerald...crowns of gold...lightnings and thunderings...seven lamps...sea of glass."

Lifted Hands

- Psalm 134:2: "Lift up your hands in the sanctuary..."

- (Not seen in heaven displays.)

Clapping

- Psalm 47:1: "O clap your hands, all ye people...."
- (Not seen in heaven displays.)

BIBLIOGRAPHY

Blomgren, David. *Song of the Lord*.
Portland, OR: Bible Press, 1978.

Boschman, Lamar. *The Rebirth of Music*.
Shippensburg, PA: Revival Press, 1980.

Piper, Don. *90 Minutes In Heaven*. Grand
Rapids, MI: Revell Publishing, 2004.

Sorge, Bob. *Exploring Worship*.
Canandaigua, NY: Bob Sorge Press, 1987.

NOTES

CHAPTER 1: PRINCIPLES OF WORSHIP

1.   Rich Nathan and Ken Wilson, *Empowered Evangelicals* (Ann Arbor, MI: Vine Books, 1995), 53.

2.   Lamar Boschman, *The Rebirth of Music* (Shippensburg, PA: Revival Press, 1980).

CHAPTER 3: DANCING, BANNERS, AND NEW SONGS

1.   Debbie Roberts, *Rejoice: A Biblical Study of Dance* (Shippensburg, PA: Destiny Image Publishers, 1982).

2.   Don Piper, *90 Minutes in Heaven* (Grand Rapids, MI: Revell Publishing, 2004).

CHAPTER 4: THE PROPHETIC ARTS

1.   Lamar Boschman, *The Rebirth of Music* (Shippensburg, PA: Revival Press, 1980).

2.   W. T. Wallace, "Memory for Music," *Journal of Experimental Psychology: Learning, Memory, and Cognition*, 20 (1994): 1471–1485.

3.   Dr. David Blomgren, *The Song of the Lord* (Portland, OR: Bible Press, 1978).

ABOUT THE AUTHOR

MARK IS A graduate of Biola University with a BA in Bible and music. Through the years, he has been in ten churches working as a chief musician and/or keyboardist in a volunteer capacity for the worship teams.

He and his wife, Patricia, have also co-led worship. Having attended fourteen worship conferences, Mark has a strong grasp of church worship principles and the presence of God in worship. In this book, he shares the knowledge he has received and experiences of corporate worship.

CONTACT THE AUTHOR

Thax49er@yahoo.com